Real Science-4-Kids

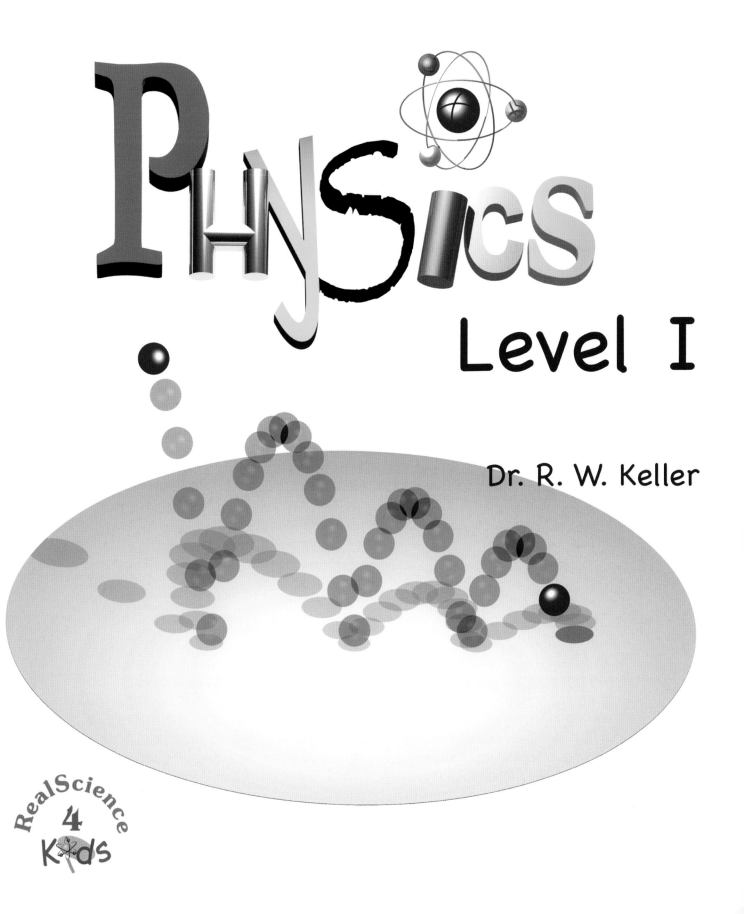

Physics

Level I

Dr. R. W. Keller

RealScience
4
Kids

Cover design: David Keller
Opening page: David Keller
Illustrations: Janet Moneymaker, Rebecca Keller

Real Science-4-Kids: Physics Level- I Textbook

ISBN # 0-9749149-4-0

Published by Gravitas Publications, Inc.
P.O. Box 4790
Albuquerque, NM
87196-4790
www.gravitaspublications.com

Printed in Hong Kong

Graphic on title page:

Energy and a Bouncing Ball -- At the top of every bounce the ball has all potential energy and no kinetic energy. As it falls it loses potential energy and gains speed until, just before it hits, it has all kinetic energy and no potential energy. However, each time the ball hits the ground, it loses some energy (as sound and heat), so each bounce is lower and lower.

Contents

Chapter 1 : What is Physics?

1.1 Introduction

Have you ever wondered what makes a feather float but a boulder fall or why a bird can fly but a whale cannot? Have you ever noticed that when your mom quickly puts on the brakes the car stops, but your ice cream ends up on the dashboard? Or have you ever wondered why, when you slide your stocking feet on the carpet, you can "shock" your dad?

All of these observations, and others like them, begin the inquiry into the field of science called physics.   The name physics comes from the Greek word physika, which means "physical or natural." Physics investigates the most basic laws that govern the physical or natural world.

1.2 The basic laws of physics

What is a basic law of physics? Are the laws of physics like the laws that tell us not to speed or not to steal? No. In fact, physical laws are statements that tell us about how the physical world around us works. Using them, we can understand why baseballs go up and then come down, why airplanes can fly, why rockets can land on the moon and why we see rainbows after it rains. Physical laws are never broken, unlike laws that tell us not to speed or not to steal.   For example, Newton's Law of Gravity tells us why we stay firmly on the surface of the earth and do not just fly off sometimes. People have always known that the world behaves in regular and reliable ways. For example, people have observed for centuries that the sun always rises and always sets, or that water always flows downhill, or that, if it is cold enough, water will turn into ice.   The laws of physics are statements about these regular and reliable observations.

We know that objects such as baseballs, airplanes, and people *consistently* obey the laws of physics and don't suddenly break one or two. It would be kind of hard to play baseball if every once in a while the ball hit by the batter landed on the moon.

1.3 How do we get laws?

How do we know what these laws are and how did we discover them? Did the earth come with a big instruction book that spelled out all of the laws? Not exactly. People had to figure them out on their own. Scientists use scientific investigation to discover how the world works. We will learn more about scientific investigation including the scientific method in the next section.   One early scientist that used scientific investigation and helped develop the scientific method was Galileo Galilei. Galileo was an Italian astronomer and was born in Pisa, Italy in 1564. He showed how two lead balls fall at the same rate even if one is larger than the other. He performed a famous experiment where he is said to have dropped two cannon balls off the leaning tower of Pisa. He found that, even though the two cannon balls were different weights, they landed on the ground at exactly the same time!

People still had trouble believing him and it wasn't until Isaac Newton showed mathematically why this was true that it was finally accepted.

Isaac Newton is considered to be one of the greatest scientists of all time. He is also considered the founder of physics as we know it today. He was born in 1643 in England. He was a brilliant man who figured out many laws about how objects move.   He was a great mathematician and wrote mathematical equations to describe these laws. One law that Newton discovered is the Law of Gravity. Newton confirmed Galileo's experiments and showed with mathematics just why two objects will reach the ground at the same time even if one is heavier than the other. Physical laws are often described using mathematics. The precision of mathematics is one reason physics is so powerful.

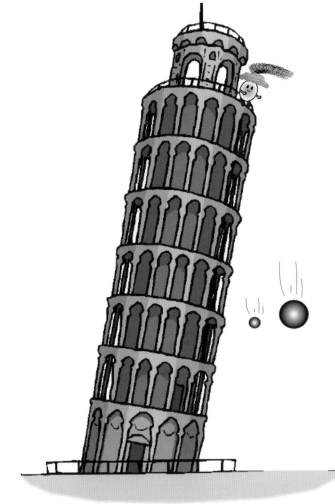

1.4 The scientific method

Newton and Galileo used the scientific method to discover the laws of motion. The scientific method is a way of gathering information and drawing conclusions based on that information. Scientists have used this method to make many discoveries.

There are essentially five steps in the scientific method. The first step is observation. A scientist, like Newton, observes how things behave and may look for patterns or things that are similar from day to day.

For example, you may notice that each time it snows, men in big trucks spread salt on the roads. You may also notice that cars have less trouble on these roads than on roads without salt.

These are observations. From these observations, you might think of a general statement that tells something about what you have observed. This is the second step in the scientific method and is called forming a hypothesis. A hypothesis is really just a guess. It is something that you think might be true about your observations, but hasn't been proven. For example, you might make the following statements about why salt is put on roads:

"The salt melts the ice on the road."
"The salt makes rubber tires sticky."
"The salt makes the snow stop falling."

All of these statements are hypotheses: that is they are *hypothetical*, meaning they haven't been proven.

The third step is to *test* your hypothesis using experimentation. By designing an experiment to test your hypothesis, you can find out

if your hypothesis is correct.   For example, you may decide to test your hypothesis that the "salt makes rubber tires sticky" with an experiment. You might take two pieces of rubber and add salt to one and not to the other. Then you would compare the two pieces of rubber to see if the one with salt is stickier than the one without salt.

This brings you to the fourth step in the scientific method, collecting results. As a scientist, you should always *record* the results of your experiment exactly as you see them. If the salty rubber is "stickier" than the regular rubber, then you should record that. If the rubber is not stickier with salt, then that is what should be recorded.   At this point, you should not let what you *think* might happen affect how you record your results.   This is

very important. Also, *everything* you observe should be written down. Even your mistakes should be recorded.

Finally, the last step of the scientific method is to draw conclusions based on what your results show. Here again, your conclusions should be based only on your results and should not be influenced by what you think *should* have happened. For example, if the salt did not make the rubber stickier, then a conclusion might be:

Conclusion:
    "Based on my data, the salt did not make the rubber more sticky. "

Based on this one experiment, you cannot say why the salt helps the cars drive more easily. You would have to conduct more experiments. But you have been able to eliminate at least one hypothesis using the scientific method. Showing which hypotheses are NOT true is often just as important as showing which one is true.

1.5 Summary

Here are the main points to remember from this chapter:

- Physics is the study of how things move and behave in nature.

- The laws of physics are precise statements about how things behave.

- The laws of physics were determined using the scientific method.

- The five steps of the scientific method are:

  1. observation
  2. forming a hypothesis
  3. experimentation
  4. collecting results
  5. drawing conclusions

Chapter 2 : Force, Energy, and Work

2.1 Introduction

What is energy? When your mom says, "I am out of energy," what does she mean? Or when you hear that there is an "energy crisis," should you worry?

Energy is actually defined as "the ability to do work." This doesn't mean that if your mom says she is out of work that she has lost her job or that a work crisis has occurred and no one is employed. Work, in this case, simply means what happens when a force moves an object.

This can seem a little confusing- so let's look at force, work, and energy in more detail.

2.2 Force

What is force? Have you ever dropped an egg on the floor? What happened? Probably you heard a noise and noticed that the egg is no longer available for your cake. In fact, you probably had to clean up a sticky mess. What happened to the egg? Why did it break? It broke because of force. The egg hit the floor with enough *force* to break it open. Or have you ever pushed on a heavy door that just doesn't seem to open? Did the door feel like it was pushing you back?   When we push on the door we apply a force to the door to open it or to move it. The door pushes back. The same thing happens when we pull on the door; the door pulls back. Both the pushing on the door and the pulling on the door are forces.

...something that changes the position, shape , or speed of an object.

There are many different sources for force. You experience one source of force every day, all day long. That is the force of gravity. The earth is the source of the gravitational force you experience. It pulls on you and makes you, and everything else, stick to the ground. The force of gravity is actually exerted by

any object. You also are a source of gravitational force, and you pull on the earth at the same time the earth pulls on you. However, because you are so much smaller than the earth, your gravitational force is small compared to the gravitational force of the earth. So, instead of dragging the earth with you out into space, the earth keeps you tightly stuck on its surface. In fact, all of the planets exert gravitational force. They pull and push each other and, as a result, balance their distances and orbits around the sun.

2.3 Balanced forces

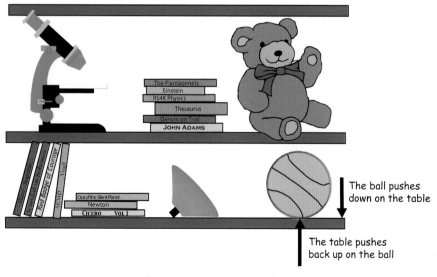

The ball pushes down on the table

The table pushes back up on the ball

Balanced forces
Equal in size -- opposite in direction

Objects that are not moving have balanced forces. For example, a toy sitting motionless on your bookshelf is actually applying a force downward toward the shelf and the shelf is applying a force upward toward the toy. The forces are balanced; they cancel each other out so the toy does not move.

Another way to look at this is to consider what happens if you and your friend are pulling a rope in opposite directions. If you both pull with equal strength and neither of you can move the other, then the forces with which you pull are equal. The forces are balanced. You both remain motionless.

Balanced forces can also occur with objects that are moving. For example, an air hockey puck slides gracefully, at the same speed, across a hockey table until it is struck with an opponent's paddle. As it is moving, and as it is at constant speed, the forces between the puck and the table are balanced. This happens with anything that slides, like snow skis, and ice skates, or even magnetic trains!

2.4 Unbalanced forces

If the forces are unbalanced, that is, one force is greater than the other, then the object will move. As long as the force keeps acting on the object, the object keeps moving faster. If the object keeps going faster and faster, it is said to accelerate. Unbalanced forces always cause acceleration. Consider if you are able to get your friend to give up, just a bit, on his end of the rope. What happens? You keep your force the same, but because he has relaxed his, BAM! He's in the puddle! Why?

Your force was greater than your friend's force and you were able to move him with this unbalanced force. When the forces were equal, you and your friend did not move. As your friend's force decreased (he relaxed), your friend began to move. In other words, he went from no speed (standing still), to some greater speed (falling in the puddle). This change in speed is *acceleration* and this acceleration was caused by a force. In this case, your pulling more strongly on your end of the rope caused your friend to accelerate into the puddle.

2.5 Work

What is work? You probably hear comments like, "I am late for work," by your dad or "I have too much work," exclaimed by your mom. You might think that work is a very grown-up thing that causes lots of stress, and your parents might agree. But in physics, work is something very simple. Work is simply the result of a force moving an object a certain distance.

When force is used to move an object a given distance, work has been done on that object. The amount of work done is calculated by multiplying the force times the distance the object has traveled.

Work = distance X force

For example, as the face of a weight lifter shows, a tremendous amount of work is needed to lift the heavy barbell from its resting position on the ground to its final position above the weight lifter's head. The amount of work the weight lifter did is proportional to the distance he has to lift the barbell. Proportional means that work and distance are related; if there is twice as much distance, the weight lifter does twice as much work.

CHAPTER 2: FORCE, ENERGY AND WORK 13

For example, a very short weight lifter would have to do less work to get the bar above his head than a very tall weight lifter. If the short weight lifter were half the size of the tall weight lifter, then he would do exactly half the amount of work.

2.6 Energy

When work has been done, and forces have been used to do that work, *energy* has been used. It's hard to define energy exactly, but one thing energy *does* is give objects the ability to do work. Take a look at the weight lifter we studied in the last section. When the bar is on the

ground, the force of pulling up on the bar to lift it above the weight lifter's head is required. When this happens, work has been done. But where did the weight lifter get what he needs to lift the bar? Wheaties! Yes! The weight lifter had to have energy in his body to use his muscles to lift the bar above his head to do work! Living things get one type of energy from food.

There are actually different kinds of energy because there are different ways to do work. The different types of energy are given different names. Some of these different types of energy are potential energy, kinetic energy, and heat energy, to name a few. We will look at these in more detail in later chapters.

2.7 Summary

- Here are the main points to remember from this chapter:

- A force is something that changes the position, shape, or speed of an object.

- Forces can be balanced or unbalanced. Objects that are not moving, or objects that are moving at constant speed, have balanced forces.

- Energy is hard to define, but it gives objects the ability to do work.

- Work = distance X force. This means that twice the distance gives twice the work for the same force.

Chapter 3: Potential and Kinetic Energy

3.1 Potential energy

What is potential energy? You've probably heard the word potential used before. For example, "He's got potential," or "The tropical storm has the potential to become a hurricane." In both of these statements, the word potential refers to something that is capable of happening or becoming. "He's got potential" simply means that he has the possibility of becoming something like a great basketball player or future leader, but he isn't one right now. The tropical storm may become a hurricane, but it isn't right now. It only has the *potential* to become one. Recall from Chapter 2 that energy is used to do work, so simply put - potential energy is energy that has the *potential to do work*.

Potential energy is a type of energy often called "stored energy." An example of something with potential energy is a book on a table. It may not seem like the book can do work, but because the book is not on the floor, it has the *potential* to fall off the table.

The book on the table has potential energy, or stored energy

The book falls and the stored energy is released

The energy released when the book falls can break the peanut-and do work

When the book falls off the table, it strikes the floor with a force. This force could be used to crack open a peanut or smash a marshmallow. The book can use the potential energy to do work.

This type of potential energy is called gravitational potential energy, because the force of gravity is required to bring it from its elevated position, on the table, to its final position, on the floor. The amount of gravitational potential energy of an object equals the amount of work that was needed to lift the object in the first place.

The amount of gravitational potential energy can be calculated by multiplying the weight of the object by the height.

gravitational potential energy = weight X height

For example, if the book is 3 feet high and weighs 1 pound, the gravitational potential energy (gpe) would be:

GPE = 3 feet x 1 pounds
or
GPE = 3 foot-pounds

3.2 A note about units

What is a unit? In physics, a unit is simply the name given to a measurement.   For example, when you measure your height, your mom might have you stand next to a wall and mark a place on the wall where your head reaches. With the ruler she will measure how tall you are by putting one end of the ruler on the floor and the other end on the mark on the wall. Your height might be something like 4 feet, 2 inches. "Feet" and "inches" are called units.

Feet and inches measure how long something is, but other units may tell us how much something weighs, like pounds or how much liquid something has like gallons. Time also has units, like hours minutes or seconds. It tells us how long something takes to happen, like how long it might take for an egg to reach the ground if it dropped from a tall building.

In the United States, we often use what are called English units, like feet and inches. But most scientists use metric units. Metric units are usually easier to work with than English units because they can be evenly divided by 10. English units are usually converted to metric units for science. The table shows some units both in metric and English.

English		Metric	
1 inch	-	2.54 cm	0.00254 m
1 ft	12 inches	30.48 cm	0.03048 m
1 mi	5280 ft	1609 m	1.609 km

3.3 Types of potential energy

There are actually several different types of potential energy. We already saw gravitational potential energy, which is energy associated with the position of an object, but there is also nuclear potential energy, elastic or strain potential energy, and chemical potential energy, and several others.

Nuclear potential energy is the energy that is stored in an atom. Nuclear reactors use nuclear potential energy stored in uranium atoms to heat water which can be used to make electrical energy (see Chapter 5). Nuclear reactors can provide electricity for very large communities and even whole countries! Elastic or strain potential energy is the energy stored in an extended rubber band or a compressed spring, and chemical potential energy is the energy that is stored in molecules, such as those found in batteries, fuels, or foods.

3.4 Energy is converted

What happens to the potential energy of the book, or the battery, or the rubber band once the energy is released? Is it still potential energy? No. The potential energy of the book, the battery, and the rubber band have all been released and converted into another type of energy. It is important to know that potential energy is useful (can do work)...

...only when it has been converted into another form of energy.

Can you think of other uses for batteries -- tree decorations perhaps or maybe

a nice hood ornament? Not really. In fact, batteries are useless unless they are actually used to light a flashlight or power a CD player. When a battery is used to power a CD player or a flashlight, the *chemical potential energy* inside a battery is released by chemical reactions and converted to electrical energy which can then be converted into light energy for the flashlight, or mechanical energy for a CD player.

3.5 Kinetic energy

We saw in the last section that potential energy must be converted into another form of energy before it can do work. What kind of energy is it converted into? When the book was dropped from the table, the gravitational potential energy was first converted into kinetic energy before it could do work on the peanut.

What is kinetic energy? The word kinetic comes from the Greek word *kinetikos*, which means "putting into motion," so kinetic energy is the *energy associated with things that are moving*. The potential energy of the book on the table is converted into kinetic energy when it falls -- that is, while it is moving toward the floor. The book has no kinetic energy as it is on the table, only potential energy.

When the book is moved from the table and begins to fall, the potential energy is converted into kinetic energy. The more it falls, the more kinetic energy it gains and the more potential energy it loses.

By the time it hits the floor -- all of the potential energy has been converted into kinetic energy. The total amount of energy has not changed -- only the form of energy. Physicists say that the total energy is conserved. That is, all of the potential energy has been converted into another form of energy. Energy is never lost -- only converted. We will learn more about the conservation of energy in Chapter 10.

How much kinetic energy does the book have? It depends. The kinetic energy of an object depends on two things -- one is the mass of the object and the other is the speed of the object.   We will learn more about mass in Chapter 4. What we need to remember about kinetic energy is:

*for a certain speed, the more mass an object has
the more kinetic energy it has.
and
for a certain mass, the more speed an object has
the more kinetic energy it has.*

So, a heavy book will have more kinetic energy than a lighter book at the same speed. Also, a book that is thrown will have more kinetic energy than a book that is dropped.

3.6 Kinetic energy and work

We already saw in the last chapter that energy is the ability to do work. When a rubber band is stretched across the prongs in a slingshot, it has *elastic potential energy.* When the rubber band is released, the elastic potential energy is transferred to the pellet in the sling shot as the pellet is propelled toward the target. The pellet now has *kinetic energy.* All, or almost all, of the potential energy that was in the slingshot is now kinetic energy in the pellet.

What happens to the kinetic energy in the pellet when it hits the target? The kinetic energy is converted to another form of energy such as heat and sound. As a result, the energy is transferred to the target in the form of work as it pushes on the target.

We say that the pellet...

...*is doing work* on the target.

3.7 Summary

Here are the main points to remember from this chapter:

- Potential energy is energy that has the potential to do work.

- A book on a table has *gravitational potential energy.*

- The energy in a stretched rubber band is called *elastic potential energy.*

- Potential energy can do work only when it is converted into another form of energy, like kinetic energy.

- Kinetic energy is the energy of motion.

Chapter 4: Motion

4.1 Motion

What is motion? We saw in the experiment for Chapter 3 that we could turn gravitational potential energy, GPE, into kinetic energy, KE, by placing a toy car on the top of a ramp, releasing the toy car, and allowing it to roll down the ramp. When the toy car rolled down the ramp, it was in motion. We learned in Chapter 3 that kinetic energy is the *energy of motion*.

We see things moving every day. All sorts of things move. Cars move down the road, planes move in the sky, we move as we work and play. Moving seems like a very ordinary thing. However, figuring out exactly how things move was a problem for early scientists. Once people started trying to figure it out, it took nearly 2000 years to finally understand!

The first person to study the science of motion was Aristotle. Aristotle was a Greek philosopher who was born in Stagira in 384 B.C. Aristotle thought that everything that was moving, like a ball, was being constantly pushed from behind. He thought that the air in front of the ball was being separated as the ball moved and that the air behind would close up forcing the ball forward. He also thought that all objects that were moving, moved because of this constant force. Because of this, he thought that since he didn't feel the earth moving, the earth was sitting still. He also thought that the sun and stars, because they changed places in the sky, were moving around the earth. Because of this he believed in a geocentric cosmos. Geo is the Greek word for earth, and centric means central. So geocentric means "earth centered."

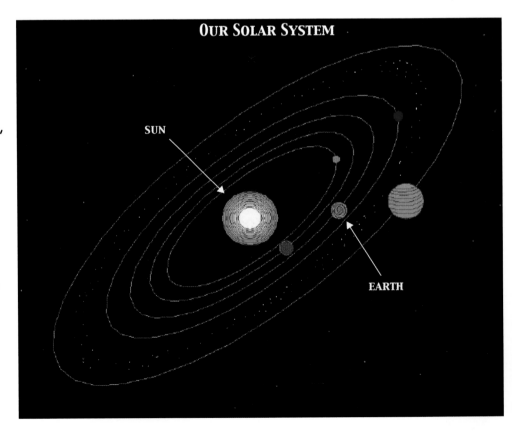

OUR SOLAR SYSTEM

SUN

EARTH

Cosmos is the Greek word for universe, so a geocentric cosmos means "earth-centered universe." Today we know that the earth moves around the sun. We know that our solar system is heliocentric, or "sun centered." [helios is the Greek word for sun]. But we didn't always know this and it took almost 2000 years from the time of Aristotle to figure out that he was wrong. It was Galileo that finally showed with experiments that motions did not require a constant force to keep them going. Later Isaac Newton put these concepts into mathematical terms.

4.2 Inertia

So, if there is nothing pushing on the ball as it travels through the air, as Aristotle thought, how does it keep going? What keeps the ball moving at all? What Galileo discovered was that things always keep moving unless something stops them. This property is called inertia [in-er-sha].

Simply put, inertia is

> *the tendency of things to resist a change in motion.*

This means that once something is moving, it will not stop, slow down, or change its

direction unless something pushes on it. So Aristotle had it completely backwards! It's not that forces *keep* things moving, but that forces stop or change things that are moving!

Everything has inertia, no matter what it is -- an atom, a rock, a baseball, or a car. Once it gets going, it won't stop or even change direction unless something pushes on it.

4.3 Mass

The property that gives things inertia is called mass. Everything has mass, and so everything has inertia. Because the force of gravity is constant everywhere on earth, you can tell how much mass something has by weighing it.

For example, a marble has less mass than a baseball because a marble weighs less than a baseball, and a baseball has less mass than a bowling ball because a baseball weighs less than a bowling ball.

We know that once rolling, a marble would be much easier to stop than a baseball, and a baseball would be much easier to stop than a bowling ball. Can you imagine trying to bowl with marbles, or trying to play marbles with bowling balls? The marbles don't have enough mass to knock down the pins and the bowling balls have too much mass to roll with your thumb!

4.4 Friction

So, if inertia keeps things moving, what makes things stop? If you roll a ball, or push a toy truck, or take your foot off the gas in your car, the ball, the truck, and the car all eventually stop moving. Why? If Galileo was right and inertia keeps things going, then wouldn't everything keep going all the time? Why do things stop?

What Galileo discovered is that objects keep going *if no forces act on them*. However, everyday objects like cars, bowling balls, and toy trucks almost always have forces acting on them. The force that makes objects stop is called friction. Friction is a force that tends to slow things down.

Usually friction is caused by things rubbing against each other. For example, if you slide a hockey puck on the street, the atoms in the hockey puck rub against the atoms in the street. The rubbing of these atoms against each other causes frictional force. The rougher the two surfaces the more friction there is. If you could change the way the hockey puck contacts the street, you could reduce the friction. This is why hockey is not usually played on streets, but on ice. The ice is much smoother than the street,

and the hockey puck slides much more easily. Galileo discovered that when he got rid of friction, things would keep on going and never stop. For example, if you could play hockey in space, where there is no air and no friction, the puck would never stop! This is one of the most important discoveries in all of physics.

4.5 Momentum

Things are also harder to stop if they move fast. A baseball rolling slowly on the ground is easy to stop, but a baseball thrown by a pitcher is much harder to stop and requires a padded glove. So there are two things that make something hard to stop: mass and speed.

In physics, the property that makes things hard to stop is called momentum. It has a precise mathematical definition:

$$\text{momentum} = \text{mass} \times \text{speed}$$

You can see from this equation that the more mass something has, the more momentum it will have. Also, the faster something travels (the more speed it has), the more momentum it will have. If something has lots of momentum, it will be harder to stop than something that has little momentum.

4.6 Summary

Here are the main points to remember from this chapter:

- Inertia is the tendency of things to resist change in motion.

- Friction is a force that tends to slow things down.

- Momentum depends on both the mass of an object and its speed.

- Things with big mass have more momentum than things with little mass.

- Things with a lot of speed have more momentum than things with a little speed.

Chapter 5 : Energy of Atoms and Molecules

5.1 Chemical energy

What is chemical energy? Simply put, chemical energy is the energy that comes from chemical reactions.

We know that if we add vinegar to baking soda, a chemical reaction occurs. We can observe the chemical reaction as the properties of both the baking soda and the vinegar change. Large bubbles are produced that signify a chemical reaction has taken place.

The energy given off in chemical reactions can be used to do work. Recall that work is done when a force acts on an object. Chemical energy can be *converted* to other types of energy and can do work. Imagine what would happen if we put baking soda and some vinegar in a jug and then put a cork on top. Pretty soon the cork would POP off the jug! The gas produced by the chemical reaction of the vinegar and baking soda pushes up on the cork -- applying a force. The force produced may eventually be strong enough to pop off the cork. In this case, the chemical reaction produced gas that did work on the

Bubbles eventually
force the top off
- doing work

Bubbles from
chemical reaction

Baking soda and
vinegar

cork.

5.2 Stored chemical energy

Before chemical energy is used or converted into other forms of energy, it is stored. Stored chemical energy is called chemical potential energy. It is is called potential energy because it has the potential to do work. There are different ways to store chemical energy. Many fuels are stored chemical energy. Gasoline, for example, is a form of stored chemical energy. Coal and wood are also stored chemical energy. Coal and wood are mostly made of carbon. When coal or wood are heated, they react chemically with the oxygen in the air. When they do this, they release a large amount of stored chemical energy. The stored chemical energy is converted to heat energy (see Chapter 8) which, for a steam engine, is can be converted into mechanical energy.

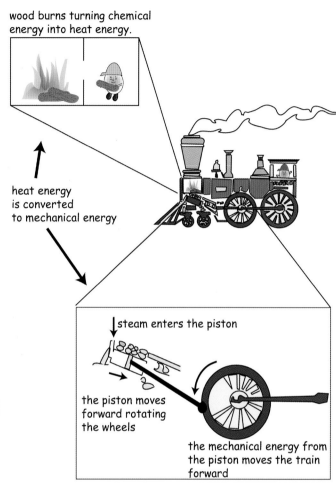

wood burns turning chemical energy into heat energy.

heat energy is converted to mechanical energy

steam enters the piston

the piston moves forward rotating the wheels

the mechanical energy from the piston moves the train forward

5.3 Stored chemical energy in food

Chemical energy is also in food. All of the food we eat is a form of stored chemical energy. Some foods, like potatoes, have lots of stored chemical energy. Recall from Chemistry Level I, Chapter 8, that the molecules in potatoes that give us energy are called carbohydrates.

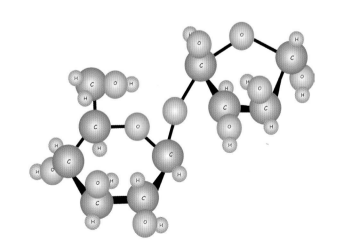

Carbohydrates are made of sugar molecules. When you eat carbohydrates your body burns the sugar molecules to release energy that the muscles in your body can use to move.   In this way, chemical potential energy in carbohydrates is *converted* to mechanical energy in your muscles.

5.4 Stored chemical energy in batteries

Batteries are another type of stored chemical energy.   The Italian scientist Alessandro Volta (1745-1827) constructed the first battery. He showed that he could generate electricity when he put two different kinds of metals in certain liquids. The first battery was made of alternating layers of silver and zinc disks separated by a cloth soaked in salt water. This is called an electrochemical or voltaic cell.   The battery generates electrical energy because the metals are

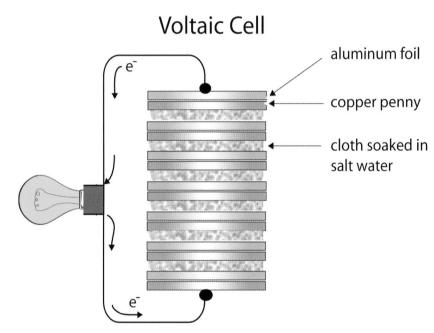

Voltaic Cell

aluminum foil

copper penny

cloth soaked in salt water

different. One metal will want to lose electrons and the other metal will want to gain them. The salt water helps the electrons travel between the metals and the wire carries the electrons through the light bulb. This is electrical energy. This is how a battery converts chemical energy to electrical energy.

5.5 Nuclear energy

Another kind of stored energy is released in nuclear reactors.   Nuclear reactors use radioactive materials to generate electricity. There is a major difference between a nuclear reaction and a chemical reaction. In a nuclear reaction the protons and neutrons get moved in and out of the nucleus. Recall from Chemistry Level I, that in a chemical reaction, only the electrons move around. When the nucleus changes, the element changes. For example, a nitrogen atom can absorb a

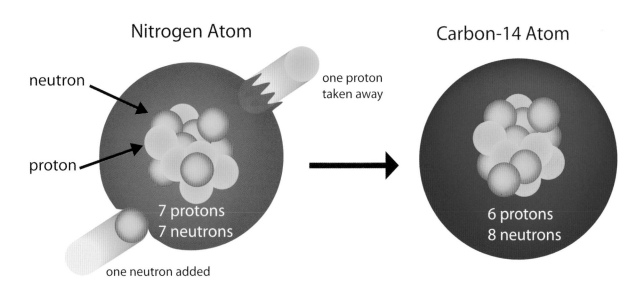

neturon. When this happens, the nitrogen ejects a proton and turns into a special kind of carbon called "carbon-14."

When a uranium atom gets hit by a neutron it does something different. Instead of losing just one neutron, a uranium nucleus will split into other elements, such as Krypton and Barium, and in the process give off several neutrons. This process is called nuclear fission.   Nuclear fission releases a huge amount of energy, much more than a chemical reaction. As little as 2 pounds of uranium fuel can produce as much energy as 2 tons of coal!

Nuclear Fission Reaction

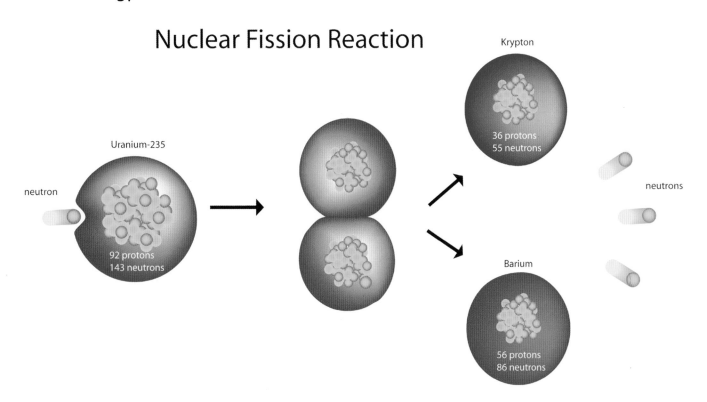

The neutrons generated can hit more uranium atoms each giving off more neutrons causing a chain reaction. This chain reaction means that there are more and more neutrons available to combine with uranium atoms and generate electrical energy.

In a nuclear reactor, the heat generated by nuclear fission is used to heat water, which makes steam. The steam then turns a turbine which generates electricity. In this way stored nuclear energy is converted to electrical energy.

Nuclear Reactor

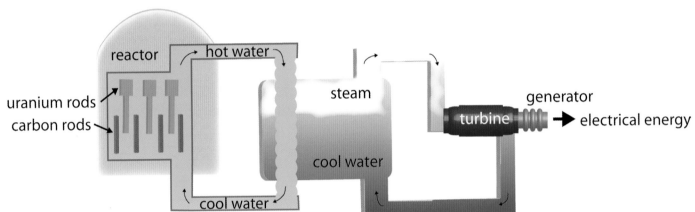

5.6 Summary

Here are the main points to remember from this chapter:

- Chemical energy comes from chemical reactioins between atoms and molecules.

- Chemical energy can be coverted to other forms of energy such as electrical energy or mechanical energy.

- Batteries generate electrical energy with chemical reactions.

- Nuclear reactors generate electrical energy using the heat from nuclear fission reactions.

Chapter 6 : Electrical energy and charge

6.1 Electrical energy

In the experiment for Chapter 5, we saw how chemical energy can be converted into electrical energy using a homemade battery. The battery we built was made by alternating layers of aluminum foil, copper pennies, and paper soaked in salt. We saw that this kind of battery was called a voltaic cell, and that the amount of voltage the battery generated was *proportional* to the number of layers in the battery.

There are also other kinds of batteries. We are all probably most familiar with a type of battery called a dry cell. A dry cell is the kind of battery that we use to put into flashlights or toy cars. A dry cell is mostly "dry" since the chemicals used are not liquids but *pastes* -- like toothpaste. A dry cell operates a lot like a voltaic cell where chemical reactions occur and release electrons.   It is the flow of these electrons through electrical wires that we call electrical energy or electricity.

Dry Cells (batteries)

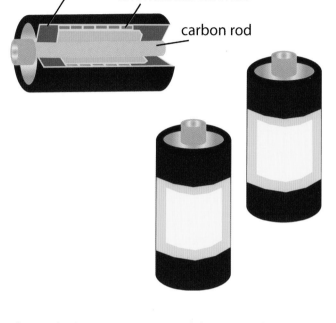

zinc   ammonium chloride   carbon rod

We see electricity at work every day. When it rains, lightning strikes because of electricity. When we turn on our lamps, we see light because of electricity. When we turn on our computers or toy cars, they work because of electricity. When we rub the family cat, its fur sticks up and sticks to us because of electricity.

6.2 Electric charge

Electricity is a general term for describing lots of different kinds of things that involve electric charge. Remember from chemistry that an electron is one part of an atom (see Chemistry Level I, Chapter 1). As it turns out, some of the parts of an atom *carry a charge*. That doesn't mean that atomic parts can go to the shopping mall and use a credit card. What it does mean is that certain types of matter attract or repel each other and, because of this, we say that these kinds of materials are charged.

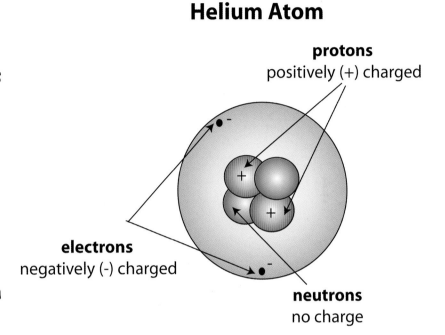

Helium Atom

protons
positively (+) charged

electrons
negatively (-) charged

neutrons
no charge

Two of the parts of an atom are charged. An electron is negatively charged and a proton is positively charged. However, a neutron does not have a charge at all -- it is *neutral*.

As it turns out, charges that are the same will repel each other and charges that are the opposite will attract each other.

So....

    1 like charges repel each other

    2. unlike charges attract each other

Two electrons that are negatively charged will try to be as far away as possible from each other. However, an electron and a proton will want to be together. Did you know that these different charges help keep atoms together? The positive charges of the protons keep the electrons from flying away from the atom!

6.3 Charging objects

Did you know that you can add or remove electrons from objects and make them charged? Using friction, you can charge yourself by sliding your stocking feet over the carpet.   Or, when you rub a balloon in your hair, you are making both

your hair and the balloon *charged* by moving electrons from the balloon to your hair. You can see this when you draw the balloon away from your hair -- your hair will begin to stick up in all directions. That's because both your hair and the balloon are now oppositely charged and so they attract each other. Your hairs are all charged with like charges so they repel each other.

6.4 Electrical force

What is it that keeps like charges away from each other and unlike charges together? It is a force called electrical force. Electrical force, like other forces, causes a change in the shape or speed of something. Electrical forces cause movements of charged particles, like electrons. They are responsible for moving electrons in wires of an electrical circuit, for the "sticking" of cat fur to the comb, and for the movement of electrons from your stocking feet to the person you shock!

6.5 Summary

Here are the main points to remember from this chapter:

- Electricity is a general term describing different kinds of things that involve electric charge.

- Atoms have charged parts. An electron is negatively charged. A proton is positively charged.

- Like charges repel each other.

- Unlike charges attract each other.

- Objects, such as balloons or cats, can become charged by adding or removing electrons using friction.

Chapter 7 : Moving Electric Charges and Heat

7.1 Moving electric charges

We saw in the last chapter that electrons and protons are charged. We also saw that like charges will repel each other and unlike charges will attract each other. Finally, we saw that we can move charges from one object to another by friction. This kind of electricity is called static electricity. The word static comes from the Latin word *stare* which means "to stand." So static electricity is electricity made of "standing charges." That means that once charges move from the cat to the plastic comb, they tend to stay there.

But electric charges can also *flow*. In fact, electric charges flow in wires much like water flows in a garden hose. When you plug in your radio, it's like hooking the garden hose to the faucet. When you turn on your radio and it lights up and you hear the music, it is like turning on the faucet and letting the water go through the garden hose. The electric charges *flow* from the outlet to your radio and back to the outlet just like the water flows through a garden hose. Flowing electric charge is called electric current.

What happens when you turn the water off? Does the hose keep flowing water? No -- except for the few drips that fall out, the hose does not continue to flow water. In fact, if the hose is on the ground, the water that is left inside the hose stays inside and doesn't come out. Why? It stays inside the hose because there is nothing pushing the water out. To make the water come out of the

hose there needs to be something pushing on the water and that something is called pressure. Pressure forces the water out, but without pressure the water just sits there.

The same is true for electric charges to flow. In order for electric charges to flow through a wire, there must be some pressure -- some "electrical pressure." This electrical pressure is called voltage. When we measured the voltage of our batteries, we were measuring how much electrical pressure they have. Batteries with large voltages have lots of electrical pressure and can move more electrons through wires than batteries with smaller voltages and less electrical pressure. However, unlike the water hose, the electrons are already in the metal wire.

When you plug your radio into the electric outlet of your home, you are providing the "electrical pressure" to move the electrons around that are *already in the wire*.

Only the electrons in an atom can move. Protons cannot move. Recall from Chemistry Level I that electrons orbit the nucleus of the atom and protons stay inside the atomic core. Some of the electrons that orbit atoms are free to move, but protons aren't. Protons stay firmly placed in the atomic core. But electrons can move, in and out of the orbits of other atoms of certain materials.

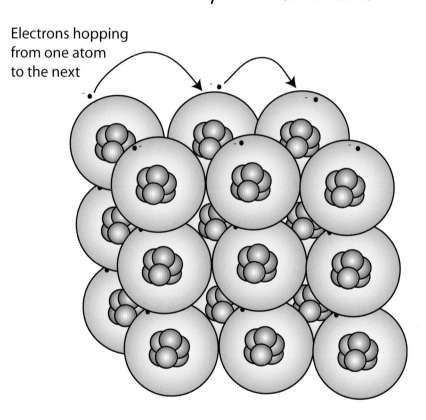

Electrons hopping from one atom to the next

Conducting Material

7.2 Resistance

We have seen how electrons travel through wires - by hopping from atom to atom. Materials that allow electrons to hop from atom to atom are called conductors.

However, some materials don't allow electrons to hop from atom to atom and these are called insulators. But why do some materials allow atoms to hop and others don't? Why are some materials conductors and others insulators? As it turns out, some materials are resistant to allowing electrons to hop from atom to atom. The word resistance comes from the Latin word *resistere*, which means "to stand [still]." So, to resist something means to stand against, or refuse to do something.

Are you resistant to eating brussels sprouts or spinach casserole? There are probably many reasons why you don't want to eat brussels sprouts or spinach casserole, like maybe you don't think they taste good, but another reason might be that you are just too full! The same is true for electrical resistance. Insulators, like foam or plastic, won't allow electrons to hop from atom to atom because they don't have extra space in their atoms to accommodate new electrons. Their atoms are too full. Other materials, called semi-conductors, allow electrons to move from atom to atom, but only under certain conditions. Semi-conductors are only partially resistant.

You can see that the more resistant a material is, the less electric flow that material will have. Partially resistant materials, or resistors, are used in electrical circuits to control the amount of electric charges that are flowing. They are used to slow down the flow of electrons in some places in a circuit.

7.3 Heat

What happens when you touch a wire that is hooked up to a small battery? You might feel some heat. The heat you feel in the wire is caused by the electrons bouncing and bumping around in the wire. For a given voltage, the less resistant the material is, the more heat it generates. This is because the less resistant material will have more electrons moving about bumping into atoms and other electrons -- which makes the temperature increase in the wire.

Heat is actually the transfer of energy from one object to another. Your fingers feel heat when they touch the wire because the temperature in the wire is greater than the temperature of your fingers. Heat energy flows from the wire to your fingers and you feel heat. If you touch an ice cube, heat energy will flow from your fingers to the ice cube and the ice cube will feel cold.

It turns out that some of the electrical energy is "lost" by heat. That means that some of the electrical energy that flows through a wire gets converted into thermal energy. Thermal energy is the energy that you can feel as heat flows from the wire to your fingers.

7.4 Summary

Here are the main points to remember from this chapter:

- Standing electric charge is called static electricity.

- When charges move or flow, they create an electric current.

- Electrical pressure is called voltage.

- Conductors allow electrons to hop from atom to atom.

- Insulators don't allow electrons to hop.

- Resistance is the tendency of a material to not allow electrons to hop.

Chapter 8 : Magnets and Electromagnets

8.1 Magnets

There are some objects that attract or repel other objects that aren't charged. These objects are called magnets. Magnets are usually made of iron or nickel. Magnets are said to have poles.

Poles are opposite, just like positive and negative charges. Magnetic poles are caused by electric charges that are *moving*. The electric charges that are moving are actually electrons *spinning* very fast on their axes around the nucleus of the atom.

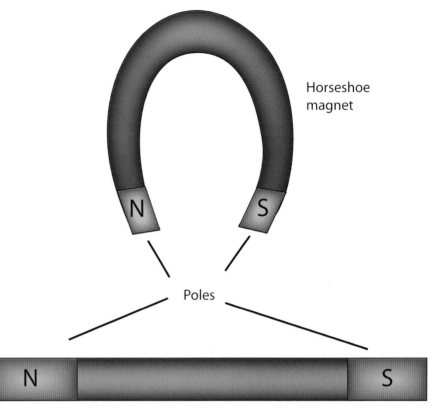

Horseshoe magnet

Poles

Bar magnet

How does this work?

Well, an electron can spin in either direction much like spinning a basketball on your finger. Like a basketball, an electron can spin to the right or to the left.

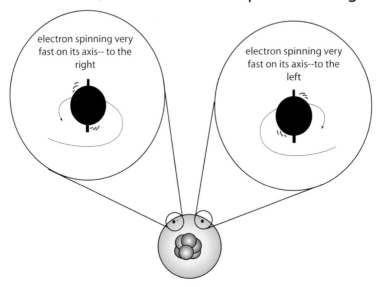

electron spinning very fast on its axis-- to the right

electron spinning very fast on its axis--to the left

The electrons on every atom in every material spin, but only some materials are magnetic. Why? Well, in materials that are not magnetic each atom has an equal number of electrons spinning both ways. That is, there is an equal number of electrons spinning to the right and to the left. But, in a magnet, there are extra electrons spinning only in one direction.

Atom with an equal number of electrons spinning in in opposite directions.

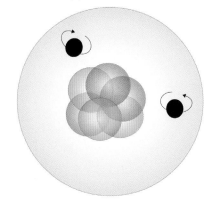

Not a magnet

Atom with an unequal number of electrons spinning in in opposite directions.

A magnet

In a magnetic object, such as a bar magnet, all of the extra electrons in each atom line up, or align themselves, making the whole material magnetic. This creates the poles we can observe when we bring two magnets close to each other.

The forces that magnets have are similar to electrical forces. Although poles are not charged they behave similarly to electric charges in that they attract and repel each other. The same rule applies for magnets that we saw

Extra electrons spinning in the same direction

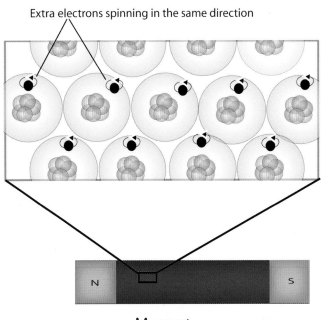

Magnet

for electric charges -- except the word "charge" is replaced with "pole":

1) Like poles repel.

2) Unlike poles attract.

However, magnets are also different than electric charges because magnetic poles cannot be separated. Recall that we could separate electric charges by using friction. We could wipe a silk cloth across a plastic rod and make the rod "charged." But we cannot separate magnetic charges. Friction won't work, and even if you cut the magnet in half, there will still be two poles on each half! You could keep cutting and cutting but even the smallest piece you cut would still have two poles. You cannot separate the poles of a magnet. This is because the atoms themselves behave like little magnets.

8.2 Magnetic fields

Both magnetic and electric forces produce what are called "fields."   A "field" simply means that the space surrounding a magnet or an electrically charged object will be affected somehow by the magnetic or electric force. Electric fields are produced by any charged object, whether moving or stationary. Magnetic fields are produced only by moving charges; stationary charges do not produce magnetic fields. The faster the charges move, the greater the magnetic or electric field.

We can see magnetic fields in the space that surrounds them. We can see "field lines" if there are objects that will move because of the fields. This is very easily observed using a magnet and iron filings.

Magnetic field lines shown by iron filings

Magnetic fields pass through most materials without affecting them. That is, you can place a magnet on your hand and the magnetic field will pass right through your hand without exerting any forces. However, magnetic fields do affect some metals -- like iron. If you take a magnet and place it close to an iron nail, the nail will become "magnetized." The magnet makes the extra electrons in the iron nail align in one direction. Unless a strong magnet is used, the iron nail won't be magnetized very much but it will be slightly magnetic and can pick up other iron nails.

This is called *inducing* a magnetic field. The iron nail wasn't magnetic to begin with, the magnet induced the iron nail to align all of its extra electrons to spin in one direction. This is called "magnetic induction."

8.3 Electromagnets

Anytime an electric current flows through a wire it creates a magnetic field around it. A coil of wire with a current flowing through it behaves much like a bar magnet. So, you can make a magnet, called an electromagnet using just a battery and wire. If you take an iron rod, place it inside the coil of wire, and hook it to a battery, the iron rod will become an even stronger magnet.

Electromagnets can be very strong, so strong, in fact, that they are used in junkyards to lift heavy cars. However, unlike regular magnets, electromagnets can be turned "on" and "off" by simply turning on or off the electricity in the wire. Once the electricity is gone, the magnetic fields are turned "off." This can be very useful for junkyards!

8.4 Electromagnetic induction

If electric currents (electric charges flowing in wires) can induce metals to become magnetic, can magnetic objects induce wires to flow charges? Yes! In fact, they can!   This is called electromagnetic induction. When a magnet is moved up and down inside a coil of wire, it produces electric current. The electric current can be measured on a voltmeter. When a magnet is pushed through the coil, the electrons in the wire move back and forth. This back and forth motion of the electrons produces an electric current. The more loops in the coil, the more electric current is produced. In fact, twice as many loops makes twice as much voltage. Also, the faster you push the magnet through the coils, the more voltage you make.   Electromagnetic induction is used to generate electricity for whole cities! In fact, the electricity that flows in your house and into your stereo is probably generated by electromagnetic induction in giant, spinning magnets in electric power plants.

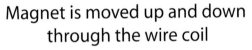

Magnet is moved up and down
through the wire coil

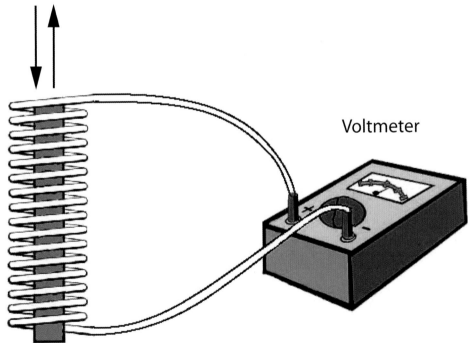

Voltmeter

8.5 Summary

Here are the main points to remember from this chapter:

- Magnets have opposite poles.

- Like poles repel each other.

- Unlike poles attract each other.

- Poles are caused by spinning electrons.

- Poles cannot be separated like charges can.

- Electromagnetic induction is the generation of electric current by moving a magnet up and down inside a coil of electrical wire.

Chapter 9 : Light and Sound

9.1 Light

What is light? We know that during the day all of our light comes from the sun. Also, in our modern world, at night we get light simply by turning on a light switch in our homes, or in earlier times, by burning a candle or lighting a fire. But what is light?

It may seem hard to believe, but light is just a combination of electric fields and magnetic fields. We saw that moving charges can produces both electric fields and magnetic fields -- so it is moving charges that produces light.   As it turns out, if we combine electric fields and magnetic fields in just the right way, we get light. The combination of the electric field and the magnetic field that makes light is called an electromagnetic wave.

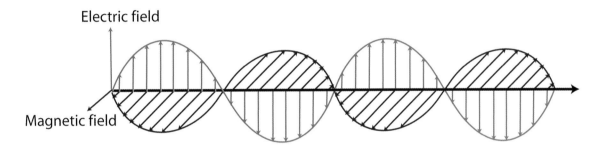

Electromagnetic Wave

9.2 Waves

What is a wave exactly? You are probably familiar with waves. In fact, if you throw a rock into a pond, you can see a ripple of water move outward in the form of small waves. What are the parts of a wave? If you look closely at the wave you've created with the rock, you can see that there are little "peaks" on top of the wave and "valleys" in between the peaks. Also notice that the peaks and the valleys repeat and that each peak is a certain distance from the other peaks. All waves are made up of several parts -- a peak, a valley, and a spacing between the peaks.

If we had to draw a wave on a piece of paper, it might look something like this:

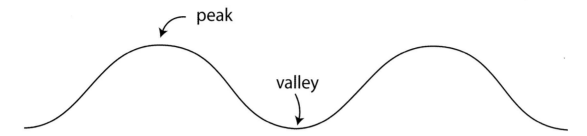

Taking a closer look at the wave, we can see peaks and valleys and space between each peak. Cutting the wave in half, lengthwise, we can label some of these parts. The height of the wave from the middle is called the amplitude and the distance between the peaks is called a wavelength.

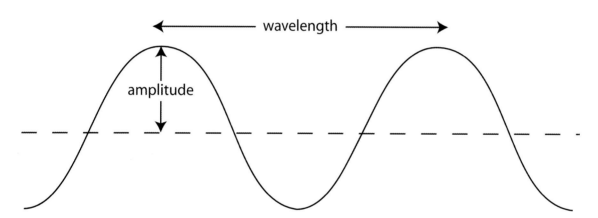

We can see that if we stretch out the wave, the distance between the peaks grows.

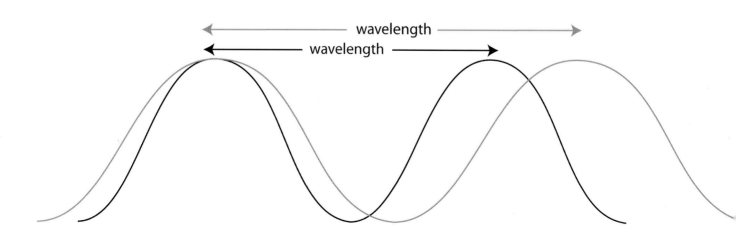

And, if we squeeze the wave together, the distance between the peaks decreases.

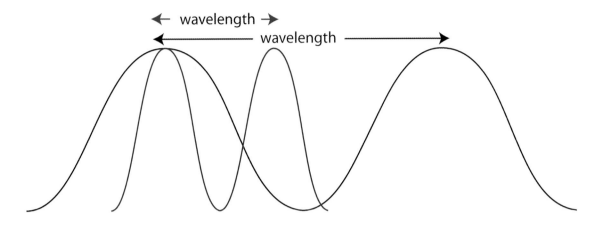

Every color of light is an electromagnetic wave with a different wavelength. For example, red light has a longer wavelength than blue light as we will see in the next section. Some kinds of light can't be seen at all. Radio waves, microwaves, and infrared light have wavelengths too long for our eyes to see. Ultraviolet, X-rays, and gamma rays have wavelengths too short for our eyes to see. We call the electromagnetic waves classified according to wavelength the electromagnetic spectrum. The electromagnetic spectrum looks like this:

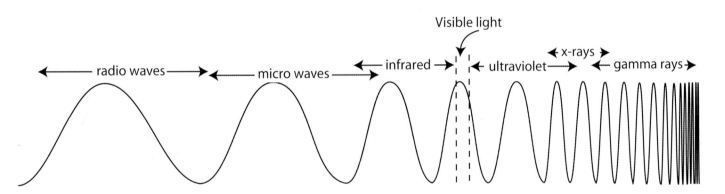

You can see from this drawing that microwaves, radio waves, and infrared light are longer than visible light. Ultraviolet rays, X-rays, and gamma rays are shorter than visible light. We cannot see waves like X-rays or microwaves. We can only see visible light. However, did you know that certain animals can see some infrared light? Foxes, cats, and other animals that see well in the dark actually see infrared light. Heat gives off infrared light and certain animals can see this heat. Scientists have made special kinds of binoculars and cameras that pick up infrared light. The special "night vision" glasses that the military use see this infrared light -- just like foxes.

9.3 Visible light

We cannot see infrared light like foxes and we cannot see ultraviolet light. However, the human eye can see a certain range of wavelengths in the electromagnetic spectrum called visible light.

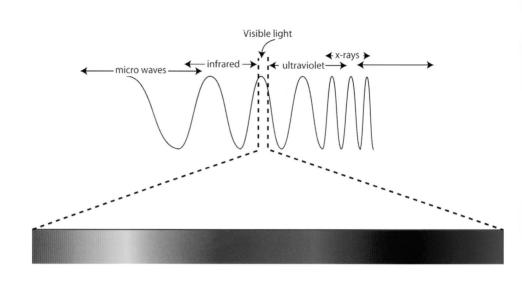

If we look carefully at the visible part of the spectrum, we find that visible light

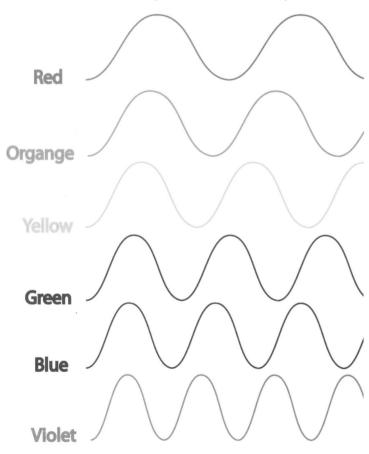

is made of many different waves at different wavelengths. As it turns out, the different wavelengths are the different colors we see. Red light has the longest wavelength in the visible spectrum and violet light has the shortest wavelength. Orange, yellow, green, and blue are in between red and violet. It is important to realize that the colors merge. For example, by taking the wavelength of red and squeezing it smaller, it turns into orange. If it is squeezed a little further, it turns into yellow, then green, and so on. This is why on the colors look like they run into each other in a rainbow, or when you look at sunlight through a prism. The colors *do* run into each other -- the only difference between them is how long or how short their wavelengths are!

9.4 Sound waves

We have seen how a rock thrown into a pond creates a wave of moving water. We have also seen that light is made of electric and magnetic fields that make a wave. What other kinds of waves are there?

Sound is also a wave. Sound is a wave of moving air. Sound waves are not electromagnetic like light. Radio waves are not sound waves. Rather, sound waves are waves of moving particles. When you pull on a guitar string or gently strike a glass with a spoon, you hear sound. That is because the guitar string and the glass vibrate, and this vibration causes the air nearby to move. The air moves in a wave just like the water in the pond.

The differences we hear in sound is called pitch. Some sounds are "high" like the sound of a whistle or chirping birds. Some sounds are "low" like that of a base drum or rumbling thunder. High-pitched sounds, like whistles or chirping birds, have high *frequencies*; and low-pitched sounds, like base drums or the rumbling of thunder, have low *frequencies*. A frequency is the number of "peaks" that pass over a given time. You can see that low pitch sounds have longer wavelengths so they will have lower frequencies for a given time than high pitches which have shorter wavelengths.

Low Pitch
low frequency sounds

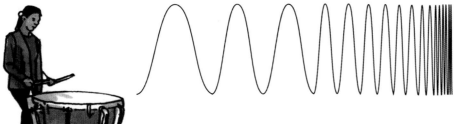

High Pitch
high frequency sounds

Sounds can also be loud or soft. This is called intensity. The intensity of a sound depends on the amplitude. The higher the amplitude, the louder the sound. The intensity of sounds is measured in a unit called a bel, named after Alexander Graham Bell who was born in 1847 in Edinburgh, Scotland but later moved to the United States. Bell invented the modern telephone using his understanding of sound and electronics. In his first successful experiment, he startled his young assistant, Mr. Watson, when from another room, he asked Mr. Watson to "come here."

Ten times the intensity of 0 bels is one bel or 10 decibels and 100 times more intensity than 0 bels is 20 decibels.   Sound intensities are usually measured in decibels. The minimum a human ear can hear, or *threshold of hearing*, is 0 decibels. A whisper is about 20 decibels and rock music is about 110 decibels. Hearing can actually be damaged above about 85 decibels, depending on the length of exposure and frequency. This is why people working around loud machinery or airports wear protection on their ears.

9.5 Summary

Here are the main points to remember from this chapter:

- Light is an electromagnetic wave made of both an electric field and a magnetic field.

- Waves have both amplitude (height of the wave) and wavelength (distance between wave peaks).

- The colors we see in visible light are made of different wavelengths; short wavelengths are blues and purples, long wavelengths are reds and oranges, and in between are yellows and greens.

- Sounds are also waves but are made of moving air.

- The frequency difference for sound is called pitch.

- Sound intensity is measured in decibels. The human ear can tolerate about 85 decibels before it is damaged.

Chapter 10 : Conservation of Energy

10.1 Introduction

Throughout these chapters, we have looked at different types of energy. We have seen *potential energy*, *kinetic energy*, *chemical energy*, and *electrical energy*. We have also seen how one form of energy can be converted into another form of energy. How *gravitational potential energy* of a toy car can be converted into *kinetic energy* and *mechanical energy* as it rolls down a ramp to smash a banana. We have seen how *chemical potential energy* inside a battery can be converted to *light energy* in a

flashlight
or

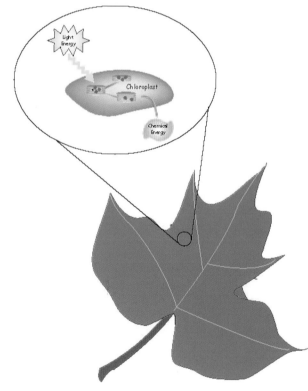

mechanical energy and *sound* in a tape player. If we recall from biology how plants make food, we can see that chloroplasts convert *light energy* from the sun into *chemical energy* in leaves. From chemistry, we saw that when we eat food, like carbohydrates, we get *chemical energy* for our bodies. When we lift a weight or run a race, this *chemical energy* is converted into *mechanical energy*.

10.2 Energy is conserved

In all of these processes, energy is neither created nor destroyed. Energy is simply converted from one form to another. In fact, energy cannot be created or destroyed, but only converted. There is a fundamental law of physics, called the Law of Conservation of Energy, which states that energy is conserved. This simply means that the total amount of energy we convert to other forms of energy is not increasing or decreasing -- but staying the same. In fact, the whole universe has the same amount of energy today that it had ten or even twenty years ago. It will have the same amount of energy tomorrow and the next day that it has today! Even in a hundred or a thousand years from now, the energy in the universe will stay the same. Energy is conserved!

How is energy conserved? In the experiment in Chapter 3, we saw how gravitational potential energy (GPE) is converted into kinetic energy (KE) when a toy car is used to smash a banana. The energy of this system, called total energy, is equal to GPE plus KE. We saw that, as the toy car rolled down the ramp, it lost GPE and gained KE. But what happened to the total energy? Did it change too? No, in fact the total energy stayed the same. We can see how this happens if we look at both the GPE and KE at several places on the ramp.

Imagine that when the car is at the top of the ramp it has 100 Joules (Joules are a unit of energy) of GPE. Because it is not moving it has no KE. When the car is halfway down the ramp, it has lost half of its GPE, but has gained KE because it is moving. In fact, it has gained the same amount of KE that has been lost as GPE. Just before the car hits the bottom of the ramp, it has lost all of the GPE, but has gained more KE. The total energy (GPE + KE) remains the same at each point. The total energy does not change. This is what is meant by conservation of energy.

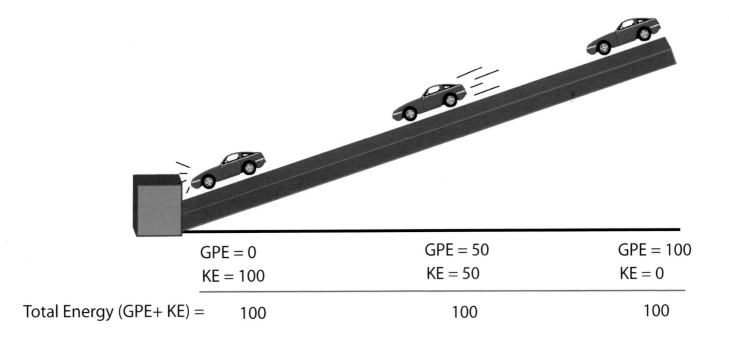

	GPE = 0		GPE = 50	GPE = 100
	KE = 100		KE = 50	KE = 0
Total Energy (GPE+ KE) =	100		100	100

10.3 Usable energy

So why is it that we often hear of an "energy crisis" or an "energy shortage?" Why are we concerned about fossil fuels or ways to save electricity? Why are we told not to "waste energy?" If we always have the same amount of energy, why do we care if we convert all of the chemical energy into light energy in a flashlight?

I BELIEVE ALL OF THE USABLE CHEMICAL ENERGY HAS BEEN CONVERTED INTO LIGHT AND HEAT.

We care because not all energy is usable energy. That is, we cannot convert all of the energy into a form that we can use. For example, when a flashlight is left turned on behind the sofa, the stored chemical energy gets converted into light energy and heat energy. The usable energy in the flashlight is "lost" when all of the stored chemical energy has been converted into light and heat energy. We can't use it anymore. In fact, we have to throw the batteries away and get new ones! But the energy isn't gone; it has just been converted into a form that we can't use. So, when someone talks about an "energy crisis" what they mean is that all of the *usable energy* is disappearing because it is being converted into unusable forms of energy like heat energy.

10.4 Energy sources

What are some of the forms of energy that we use? We've already seen that the batteries we use store chemical energy but what about other forms of energy? Where do we get gasoline, or electricity, or natural gas?

Some of the energy we use comes from fossil fuels. Fossils fuels come from dead plants and animals. When a plant or an animal dies, the

Plant fossil

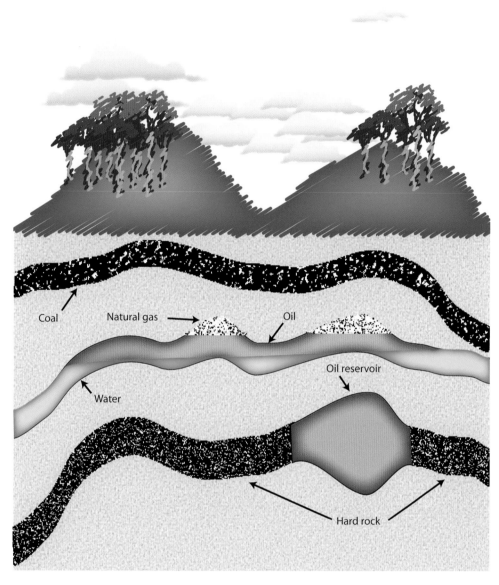

Coal

Natural gas

Oil

Oil reservoir

Water

Hard rock

tissues and cells that the plant or animal is made of *decompose* or break down into smaller pieces. One of the smallest pieces that all living things break down into is carbon. Sometimes, if the conditions are just right, the carbon from the dead plants and animals combines with hydrogen and turns into oil, coal, and natural gas. These are called fossil fuels.

Oil, coal, and natural gas are found under the ground . Oil can be trapped by certain types of rocks and form pools, also called reservoirs. Oil can be removed from a reservoir by drilling holes deep into the rocks and pumping the oil out. Oil found underground is called crude oil or petroleum. Petroleum gets turned into fuels for cars, trucks, and even planes. But it can also be turned into other things such as plastics, waxes, fibers, and dyes.

Natural gas is also formed from tiny plants and animals that have died and decomposed. Natural gas is often found in the same place as oil. Natural gas is mostly made of methane. Methane is a carbon atom with four hydrogens attached.

Coal is also found underground. It is formed by decaying plants that died a long time ago. Coal is hard and cannot be pumped out of the ground like oil. Coal must be removed by digging. Large holes or shafts, together with tunnels, are dug deep into the ground. Both men and digging equipment can then get inside the ground to remove the coal.

Coal was the main fossil fuel up until the early 1900s. It was used to power steam engines and factories and to generate heat for making steel and iron. Today coal is mostly used to generate electricity.

Coal miner underground

There are energy sources other than fossil fuels that we can use for powering cars or for electricity in our homes. Two important sources of usable energy are wind and water. Windmills harvest energy from the wind and have been used for centuries to pump water from the ground.

Even today it is common for windmills to bring water to the surface on farms and for cattle on ranches. Windmills can also be used to generate electrical energy. Wind power is a renewable energy source. This means that, unlike coal and oil, we will never run out of wind.

Flowing water in rivers is used in many places as a source of energy. Falling water from a dam has enough force to turn a turbine which generates electrical energy. A river

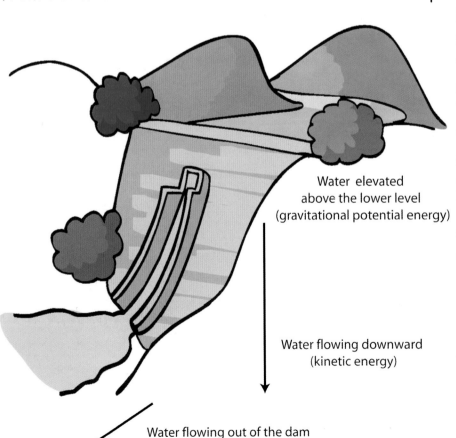

Water elevated
above the lower level
(gravitational potential energy)

Water flowing downward
(kinetic energy)

Water flowing out of the dam
(potential energy converted to kinetic energy)

can be blocked to create a reservoir of water at high elevation. Because the water is at high elevation it has gravitational potential energy. When the water is released, the potential energy is converted into mechanical and electrical energy as it passews through the turbines in a dam. The reservoir is refilled by rain or flowing rivers so flowing water is also a renewable energy source.

The sun is a very important source of energy for plants. We can also use the sun's energy to generate electricity or heat water. Solar energy can be harvested using solar panels. A simple solar panel for heating water can be made out of a black plastic sheet and glass panes fitted into a box. Solar panels that convert the sun's energy into electricity are also sometimes used in homes or on space vehicles like the space shuttle. At present, solar power is relatively expensive, and so is less used than energy from fossil fuels or flowing water. But as the technology for harvesting solar power improves, it may become cheaper and more common.

10.5 Summary

- Energy is converted from one form to another.

- Energy is conserved. This means that the total energy does not change.

- Some of our energy comes from fossil fuels like oil, carbon, and natural gas.

- Some energy can be harvested from the wind, the sun, and flowing water.

Glossary-Index

Fossil fuels ● stored energy from decomposed plants and animals such as oil, coal, and natural gas, 62, 63.

Frequency ● number of peaks in a given amount of time, 57.

Friction ● force that causes objects to slow down and stop, 26.

Galileo ● Galileo Galilei, an Italian astronomer, who studied physical laws using the scientific method, 3, 4.

Geocentric cosmos ● false belief that the earth was the center of the world, 24, 25.

Gravity ● physical law discovered by Newton. The force exerted by objects on one another. The earth's gravitational force keeps objects on its surface, 2, 4, 10.

Heliocentric cosmos ● sun-centered universe, explained by Galileo and proven by Newton, 25.

Hypothesis ● second step in scientific method - a guess about what you have observed, 5, 6.

Inertia ● tendency of things to resist a change in motion, 25.

Insulator ● material like foam or plastic that resists the flow of electrons from atom to atom, 43.

Intensity ● loudness or softness of sound based on the amplitude of the sound wave; the higher the amplitude, the louder the sound, 58.

Joule ● a unit a measure for energy. One unit of work is done when a force of one newton moves an object one meter, 61.

Kinetic energy ● [Gk. kinetikos, "putting in motion"] power involved when things are moving, 19, 20.

Law of Conservation of Energy ● see conservation of energy.

Light ● an electromagnetic wave made of both an electric field and a magnetic field, 53.

Magnet ● object that attracts or repels uncharged objects - magnets have poles that are charged by spinning electrons and extra electrons spinning only in one direction, 46, 47.

Magnetic field ● space around a magnet that is affected by the magnetic force, 48.

Magnetic induction ● power of a magnet to cause a non-magnetic object such as an iron nail to become magnetic - this happens because all of the extra electrons are forced to spin in one direction, 49.

Mass ● property that gives things inertia, 26.

Metric units ● measurements commonly used by scientists such as centimeters, liters, etc., 18.

Momentum ● property that makes things hard to stop (momentum = mass x speed), 27, 28.

Motion ● movement of objects, first studied by Aristotle, 24.

Newton ● Isaac Newton, famous scientist and mathematician; founder of physics, 2, 4.

Nuclear fission ● process that occurs when atoms split, giving off large amounts of energy, 33.

Nuclear potential energy ● power stored in an atom, 18.

Nuclear reactor ● machine that uses radioactive materials to generate electricity, 32, 34.

Observation ● first step in scientific method - this involves looking for patterns in the world surrounding us, 4, 5.

Physics ● field of science that investigates the basic laws of the natural world, 2.

Pitch ● a frequency or wavelength that causes different sounds; high-pitched sounds are caused by shorter wavelengths than low-pitched sounds, 57.

Poles ● the parts of a magnet that have opposite attrations due to electrons moving in opposite directions on their axes - like poles repel and unlike poles attract, 46, 47, 48.

Potential energy ● power to do work, stored energy, 16, 17.

Pressure ● force that moves things - like electricity through wires, 42.

Resistor ● material that slows down the flow of electrical charges, 43.

Results ● fourth step in scientific method - this involves recording what you discovered from your experiment, 6.

Scientific method ● 5 steps used by scientists to make discoveries: observation, hypothesis, experimentation, results, and conclusion, 4.

Semi-conductor ● material that is only partially resistant to the flow of electrons, 43.

Solar energy ● energy from the sun, 65.

Sound waves ● waves of moving particles - low sounds are caused by longer wavelengths and high sounds are caused by shorter wavelengths, 57.

Static ● [L. stare, "to stand"] electricity with standing charges, 41.

Strain potential energy ● see elastic potential energy.

Thermal energy ● heat, the transfer of energy from one object to another, 43, 44.

Unit ● a measure of something - units include inches, centimeters, pounds, minutes, etc., 17, 18.

Usable energy ● energy such as gasoline, electricity, or sunlight that can do work, 62.

Vibration ● slight movement which causes us to hear sound such as a guitar string being plucked, 57.

Visible light ● range of electromagnetic wavelengths the human eye can see - colors are made of different wavelengths, 56.

Volta ● Alessandro Volta, an Italian scientist who constructed the first battery called a voltaic cell, 32.

Voltage ● electrical pressure - the greater the voltage, the more power to move electrons through wires, 42.

Voltaic cell ● battery that generates electrical energy by putting different kinds of metals together with certain types of liquid, 32.

Wave ● peaks and valleys which are measured by amplitude and wavelength - some waves include sound waves, light waves, and gamma rays, 53, 54, 55.

Wavelength ● measure of the distance of a wave between peaks, 54.

Work ● this occurs when a force moves an object (distance x force), 9.